Poetry for Different Moments

Maria Thacker

BookLeaf Publishing

Presentation by *BookLeaf Publishing*

Web: www.bookleafpub.com

E-mail: info@bookleafpub.com

ISBN: 9789357613958

First edition 2022

Darkness into Light

The sun shone bright as the shadows fell down
The darkness cast away, consumed by light
And yet she stood fearful of the bright light
Was she worthy of this, she knew not why?
The light continued shining upon her
The darkness completely vanished away
She fell staring upward in amazement
This moment lasted but a minute now
Tears fell as she was wrapped in loving arms
She stood, light shining as darkness stayed back
The shadows were now a past memory
A forgotten time, she knew her full worth
The sun embraced her as she moved forward
The shadows fell as the sun shone brightly

Tetelestai

One look back was all that it took
The past, the present, the future
It all blurred together quickly
The pain, the beauty, the heartbreak
This time it was overwhelming
Falling, falling, falling, falling
Then nothing, pitch darkness fell down
The world gone silent as she lay
Overwhelming sense of despair
Two hearts beating as one heart formed
Found as old memories faded
Rising, rising, rising, rising
Made anew safe at last, fear gone
All beauty, light, love overcame

Epiphany

She walks the path of beauty and of truth
Overbearing is the despairing pain
All around she looks, but all feels lost still
The world feels different and yet nothing's
changed
The path is changing the steps seem harder
Where is the beauty and truth that once walked?
Swirling, swirling, swirling, swirling, swirling
Pitch black she hits the deep hole of her mind
Everything has changed, now there is nothing
The path once walked has vanished before her
eyes
Turning she feels dizzy and overwhelmed
Pressing forward she breaks the wall of despair
And now, if even only now, the path is found
Beauty and truth surrounds her as she walks

Shadows

Staring at her reflection staring back
The smile, the appearance, shadows of shame
Wiping a tear she turns and walks away
Why did the world change her pure innocence?
The girl she once knew is long gone away
Walking forward she puts on that fake smile
No one notices the call for help in her eyes
Alone and lost in a world of shadows
In and out she goes everyday nothing
Will she ever believe in hope again?
She looks up staring back she sees her there
A small smile appears, a glimmer of hope
Reaching out she stands and takes the child's
hand
Safe, loved, not alone, she is found again

The Mind

5

Being pulled apart this war between them
The rope is slipping, she falls exhausted
Endless days and nights, deceiving the mind
Her strength is disappearing over time
This war is taking over, consuming her
Will she win or lose? Who is to decide?
The clock of time is ticking over me
The struggle of the mind is controlling
The battle always seems never ending
The everyday back and forth is too much
Reaching for the rope one last time, she rises
The war still hanging but she's in control
Her strength regaining, she finds her balance
The war once consuming her, is lifted

Breaking the Silence

6

Words unspoken, bottled up inside her
Time stood still, her mind in utter directions
She wants to speak but they won't understand
Away she goes keeping her thoughts contained
Over and over again the unspoken words
She tries again but knows it will bring pain
Silent again she falls into her thoughts
Will she ever be free of the weight?
Feeling trapped, the space around tightening
She wants to scream but nothing will come out
Time passes by the walls moving inward
Finally it subsides she can breathe now
The thoughts flood from her mouth, she waits
for them
The pain, the anger, the love, she is free

Life

Sleepless nights of fighting back all the tears
She lies awake contemplating her life
Nothing makes sense what seemed easy is hard
She tries everything to hold it all in
Nothing can change the daily pain she feels
Everything seems to slowly fade away
All around is nothing but full darkness
The darkness pushes her deeper downward
Lying there as the world moves around her
She wonders what if things had been different
Would she take the risk and start all over?
Still unsure as the darkness is lifted
Reaching up she fades back into place now
An overwhelming peace consuming her

Satisfied

Written in the sky was words she longed for
She wished to reach them but they slipped away
Laying there in utter, complete array
Her mind like a unsettled ocean wave
Always lapping over and over her
Standing, the words lingering above her
Why can't she feel the words she longs for?
She wonders if they even care about her
Day falls into night, the words seem to change
She feels hopeless and without any purpose
Slowly she starts to drift away to sleep
She sees the words once more, this time they
stay
Everything feels different she now has hope
Her longing has settled, she feels love again

Control

Trapped in this room everyone watching me
Emotionless so as to not break them
Heavy again is the weight upon me
Nothing is changing no one listens now
They speak for you not letting you speak here
Sitting day and night watching your life go
Being controlled by a string moving you
How long will this go on? Will it end soon?
Many nights go by playing string puppet
Feeling nothing now but emptiness now
Words being continuously forced in
It's straining her emotions, will she break?
Once the puppet on the string, she collapsed
Trapped no more, her emotions pouring out

Invisible

She waits night after night for them to come
She longs to be found and truly seen in truth
They pass by but they don't see who she is
Invisible, not seeing from her eyes
Stuck she cries out but they don't see the tears
Time passes waiting to be understood
Will they ever understand the silence?
She speaks but they don't hear the silent words
Sitting in darkness she cries waiting still
Will she ever be seen in eyes of truth?

A Mother's Touch

She stands day after day waiting for you
Her love for you is beyond all compare
She watches over you with open arms
There may be days that waves crash around us
But the I love you's won't go unspoken
A mother's bond is stronger than the waves
Each day as time goes on you understand,
The way she waits for you even through the
storms
Words of encouragement and complete strength
She pushes you farther along the path
Watching as you grow up, becoming you
Arms still open to embrace you always
She waits always for you day after day
Her love is beyond comparison

Revealed

Hiding in the shadow of a mask not wanting to
be seen
Each and every glance
Lets go far away and be who we want to but
when we return we put our shield up
Is this how life is to be unseen, seen
Is there a way out to escape the hidden,
To be seen as not another face in the crowd but
as who we are deep within
Why do we put put these shields, these masks?
When can we reveal who we are deep within?

The Battle

What does it mean to be strong?
Everywhere I go I feel trapped
I just want to feel safe, to belong
Tired of fighting, of holding it together
Will this pain ever end?
How can I be okay when everything is crashing
around me?
Struggling to breathe as the pressure builds
These feelings consume me like a tidal wave
Shaking as I try to control them
Wanting to feel at peace but getting wrapped up
in others feelings
Letting go, shutting it all out as I am wrapped in
arms of peace
I feel safe, at home

Remember

Memories slowly flood in full of joy and pain
Summer days of sweets and laughter
Followed by tears, that flow like a fountain
The past pulls you in like a tidal wave
Slowly consuming you
Where is the end? The light to the tunnel?
Trying to turn back time grasping at what is left
Memories come and go like the waves in the
ocean
Every time you reach out it disappears
Wishing time would slow down
Missing what was, the sand is slipping through
my hands
Grasping holding on to what sticks
Not letting go of the memories that stay
Always remembering never forgetting

Simplicity

Sitting by a campfire the silence
Filled with quietness and simplicity
Overwhelmed with utter and complete peace
It has been a while since I have felt this
Consumed as joy fills me in this moment
Feels like I have been here for eternity
The perfection in the simplicity
Time has stopped, surrounded by the beauty
Never letting go of this moment now
Standing still lost as time around me has stopped
The fire sparks as I lay watching stars
Make a wish as the quietness lingers
Closing my eyes I take everything in
The campfire fades but this peace will last

New Things

Life is full of twists and turns, joy and pain
Taking risks or trying something new can seem
scary
Embracing the new, live life to the fullest
Be true to yourself and let what fills you with
joy take over
Being open to being honest with yourself
Life is messy but that's what is perfect
Time to go new directions see where the wind
will take me
Be brave, embracing life with new eyes
I want to soar, to fly to be free
Free from the pain, free to be me

Changing Time

Day one seems so far away but yet right around
the corner
A breath of fresh air fills me as I remember
The past full of emotions
I laugh, I cry, I long for more
Suddenly the wind takes a new course, full of
uncertainty
I feel lost, alone, helpless
I shiver in the wind as I am pushed away
This feeling of betrayal, like a dark cloud above
me
I reach out hoping to find someone who cares
Ever so gently the wind guides me back safely
A new day as familiar as day one
The sun shines through me bringing warmth
Ready to begin again

Thanksgiving

Colors surrounds me like leaves falling off a tree
Each one so different yet specially picked
As I gather at the table with loved ones I think of
those leaves
The colors all intertwined together yet each hold
a different story
It is a time to be thankful for all we have been
given
Each one of us holds a leaf that swirls in and out
of each other's life
This day is a day of thanksgiving joined as one
Even if it is only for a day before the leaves pick
up again
Floating, swaying as the wind carries them to
another path
Grateful for the day ready to join again on this
day of Thanksgiving

Anxiety

I feel like I am sinking like the sand
Each breath I take is like water consuming me
Trying to stand my ground but everything is
shifting
Grasping for anything to find balance
How do you find the strength to move on when
it feels like it is crashing around you
The waves constantly flood over me making it
hard to push forward
The ground below is shaking trying to stay a
float
I want things to go back to normal
Feeling afraid full of anxiety
The feelings of being lost, unsure of what is to
happen
Heart beating so fast, as I continue to sink
I want to feel safe, when will it be okay?

Belonging

Why is it when everything falls apart you begin
to want to start again?
The idea of falling over and over
I am torn inside by who I am and who I want to
be
The pressure is overwhelming
Going back and forth full of questions
What does it mean to belong? Who am I?
Falling into the unknown, reaching to be seen
How do I start over?
Trying to create a new path, paving a new way
Turn left, right, going around and around
Lost within as I try to find my way
I see it small at first but hopeful
No longer torn but starting to be mended
The new path full of unknowns but also full of
such certainty and peace
I belong

www.ingramcontent.com/pod-product-compliance
Lightning Source LLC
LaVergne TN
LVHW051252200726
843510LV00011B/1825